Rocket
Rill's

Golf Etiquette
For Martians

Written & Illustrated by
David J. McBride

Sidney the Martian is a gentleman who I met on my first visit to Mars. He had just invented an outdoor sport where the players, using sticks, tried to get little green rocks into a very tiny hole in the ground. He was really excited.

"That's *golf* Sidney," I explained. "On earth we call this game G-O-L-F. Golf is great because anyone can participate, even someone like me.

Allow me to introduce myself. I'm Rocket Rill, a retired astronaut. I've often been described as handicapped, though *physically-challenged* suits me better. I was born with a unique body—just a head, two arms, two hands, and one very large foot. I am especially useful because I fit really well into small areas—like space ships!"

"How often do you play?" inquired Sidney.

"Every day since retiring. I love this game. It's so much fun and the people are so nice."

"Mr. Rill, would you please join me in a game?" asked Sidney.

"I would be honored, but I didn't bring my golf instruments."

"We use sticks, Mr. Rill, big fat sticks. And we have plenty of them."

So Sidney and I flew out to a valley where he had just built a golf course with nine holes. A golf course on Mars! *Very cool* ......or so I thought.....

When we landed in the parking lot, I noticed a very loud noise coming from the clubhouse. The golfers were arguing and fighting to tee off at the same time. It was unbelievable how they were yelling, even while other Martians were still playing their shots. Many were cheating, moving their ball to better locations, and some players lied about their score. Sidney's brother, Simon, would have a tantrum and bang his stick onto the ground whenever his rock missed the hole. Not only did he damage the delicate red putting surface, he broke many of his nice sticks! At the end, the winners made fun of those with higher scores, and they argued and fought some more. It seemed like everyone was mean and cranky!

This was not the game of golf as I knew it.

"Sidney, I'm going back home. I don't feel comfortable here," I said. Sid got a sad look on his face.

"Can I come with you?" he asked. "I want to see what golf is like on Earth."

So Sidney and I started our journey back to Earth to play at one of my favorite courses, The Captain's Club, in Cape Canaveral, Florida.

"Let's hurry up and tee off," said Sidney.

"First things first, we have to call for a tee time."

After we called on our interplanetary cell phone, we obtained an 11:00 AM tee time paired with my friends, Freddie and Mel, at the Ocean Dunes Course. This was just one of two golf courses at The Captain's Club (the other course is called Lakeside). It was now 10:00 AM.

"Good, we have time for a nap," said Sidney.

"Actually Sid, here on Earth we show up early at the golf course for our tee times. This gives us time to relax in our new surroundings, loosen up our muscles, practice our full swing, as well as short pitch shots, chipping, and putting. Furthermore, we try to be *ready* when it's our turn to swing--for every shot. This we call "ready golf." It's very important to keep things moving along on the course."

"Everyone is so nice here," Sidney agreed, after checking in at the pro shop. "The people from the golf course actually cleaned my golf sticks for me, and then carried them to the first tee. And the players on the first hole asked if we wanted to go ahead of them. They were very polite."

"That's just one reason why I enjoy golf here on Earth so much. We all root for each other. The players try to be prepared for each shot, truthful about their score, and courteous to others. It's not like some of the other sports. There are no referees in this game. *You* are responsible for learning the rules, being honest and having fun."

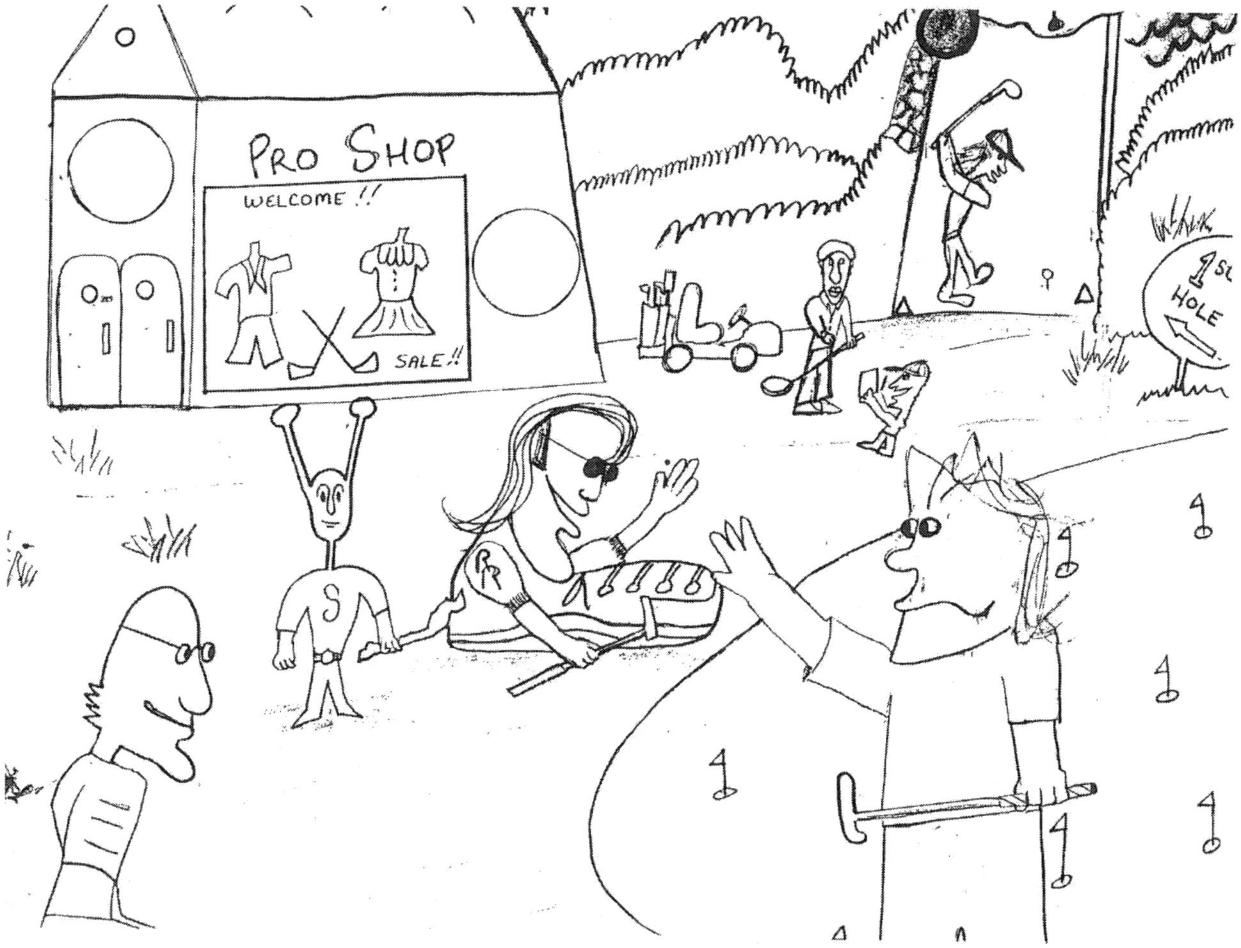
PRO SHOP
WELCOME !!
SALE !!
HOLE

So finally, at 10:55 A.M. we checked in at the first tee with the *Starter*. "Can I go first?" whined Sidney, anxious to get things under way.

"We'll flip a tee," I said, anxious to teach my new friend what golf is all about. As luck would have it, the tee pointed my way.

"Well, what are you waiting for?" barked Sidney.

"Actually, my friend, I must always wait for the group ahead of me to clear out of the way before I swing. It's courteous to do so, and more importantly, it's safe! It would be dangerous for me to hit my ball while people are still playing in front of us. Someone could possibly get hurt badly if struck by the ball. Also, while we are on the subject of safety, to protect yourself and others, never stand near someone who is swinging and never swing when someone is standing near you."

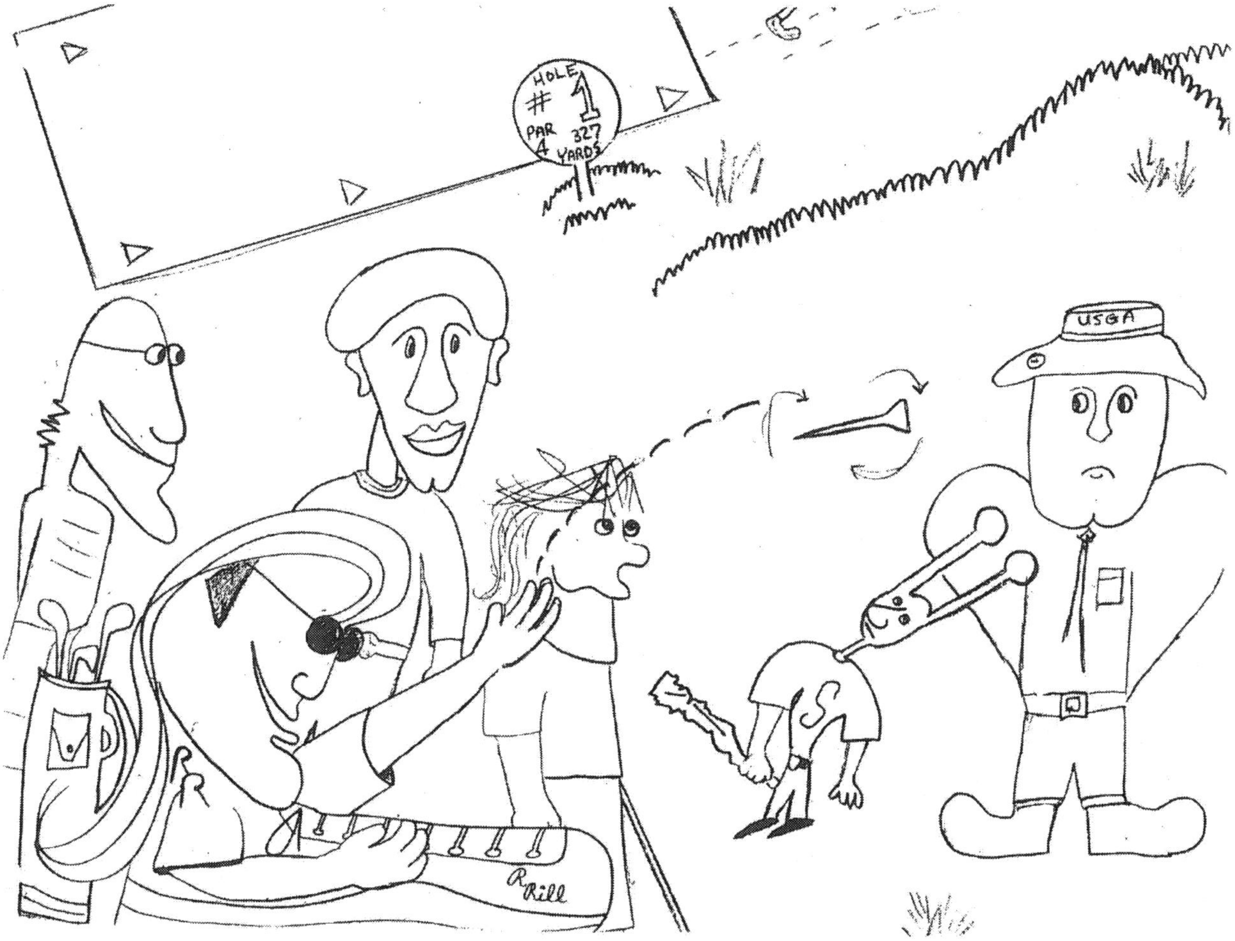
HOLE
1
PAR
4
327
YARDS
USGA
R. Rill

And so we began our round. On the second hole, Sidney, curved his ball (a slice) and it sailed into a big tree. Sidney acted like his brother, Simon, yelling and then slamming his stick into the nice green grass. Also, he never watched his ball to see where it stopped.

"If you have a temper, we'll have to leave, Sidney," I said sternly. "Golf can be difficult, and sometimes it gets frustrating, but angry outbursts and hurting the golf course is not allowed. Maybe next time you should take a deep breath and just shout out 'HOT DOG' if you get mad. It will make you feel better."

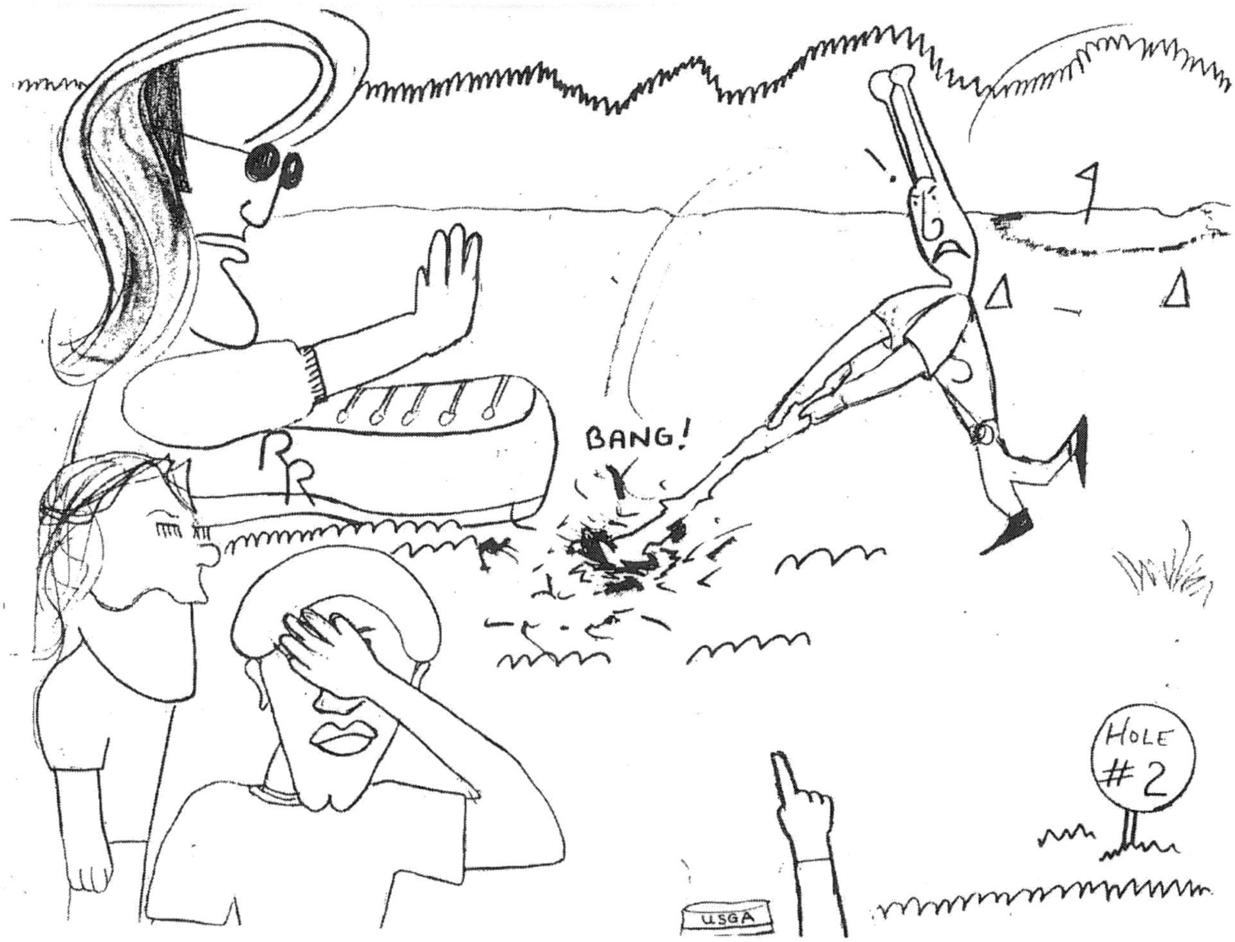
BANG!
RR
USGA
HOLE #2

"I am sorry," said the Martian, "I'm so embarrassed for getting upset and banging down my stick."

"It's okay Sidney, let's go look for your ball." So Freddie, Mel and I helped Sidney find his ball. We knew which tree it was near because we watched it roll there.

"Why are you helping me look for my ball?" asked Sidney. "No one ever helped me find my lost rocks on Mars!"

"We saw where it went while you were pouting," I said. "Besides, we only have five minutes to find your ball according to the rules, and we have to try to keep up with the group ahead of us."

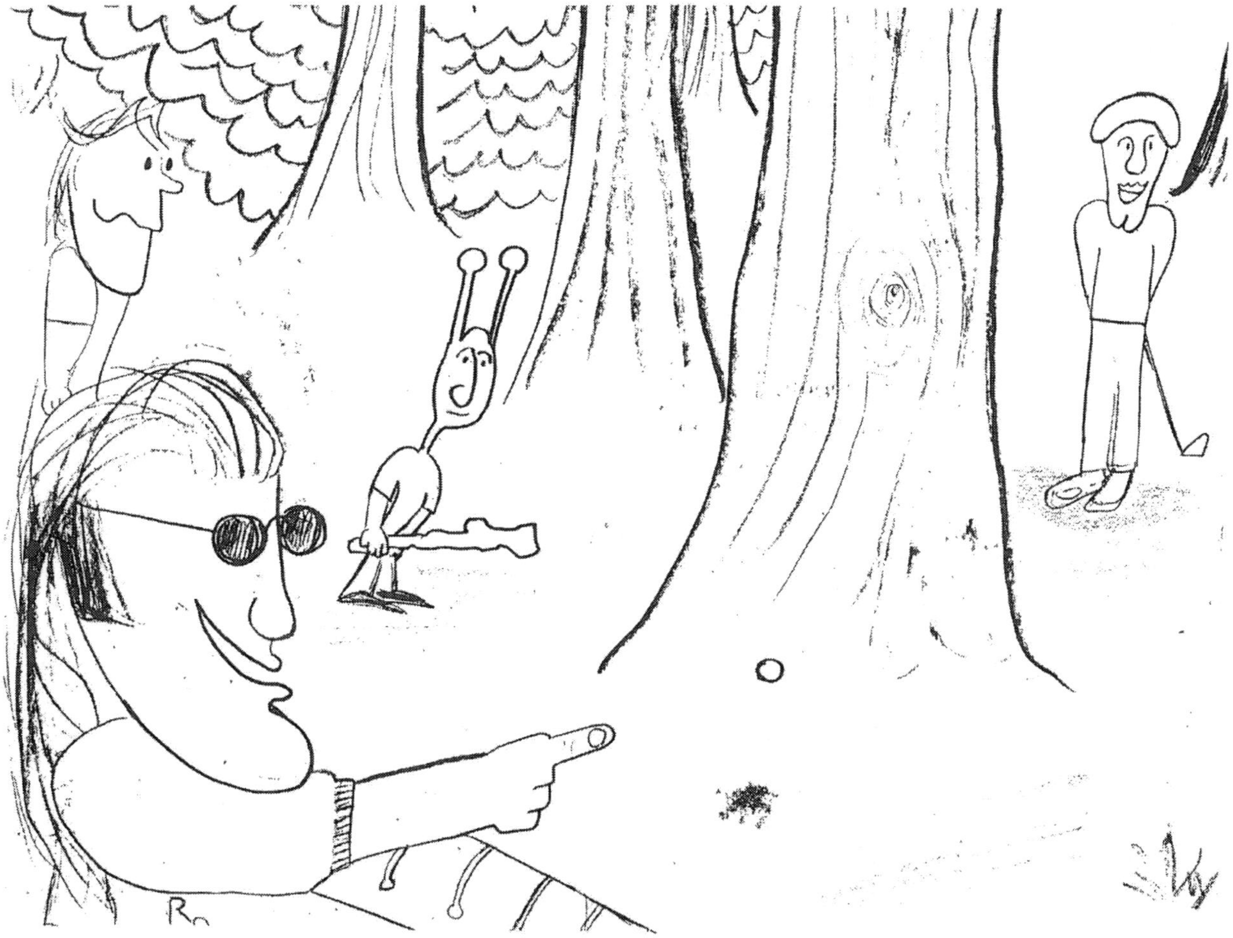

On the fourth hole Sidney curved his ball (a hook this time) over the fence and out-of-bounds. "You have to play a second ball now, Sid, called a 'provisional' ball. You should always do this when you think your ball could be lost or out-of-bounds," I explained. I was keeping score today for our foursome, and with Sidney in the group that was no small task. I should have brought my calculator.

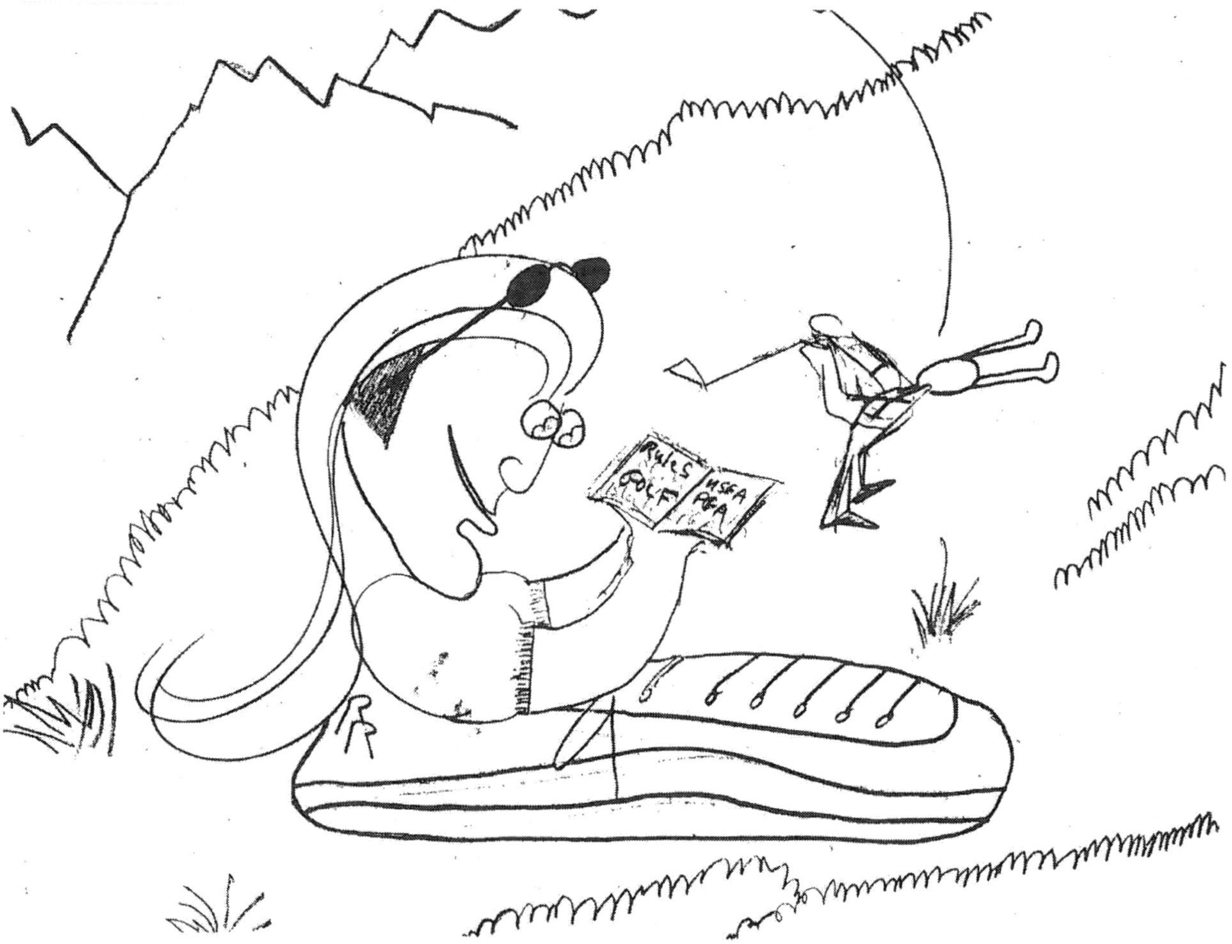
Rules
GOLF
USGA
PGA

For the first eight holes we put up with Sidney's *alien* behavior. He was constantly talking and moving around when others were preparing to swing. On the greens, he would walk in the paths of our imaginary putting lines, accidentally leaving footprints. And when he finally got his ball into the hole and was taking it out, Sid would damage the edge of the cup by stepping too close. I couldn't take it any more.

"Sidney, we have to talk."

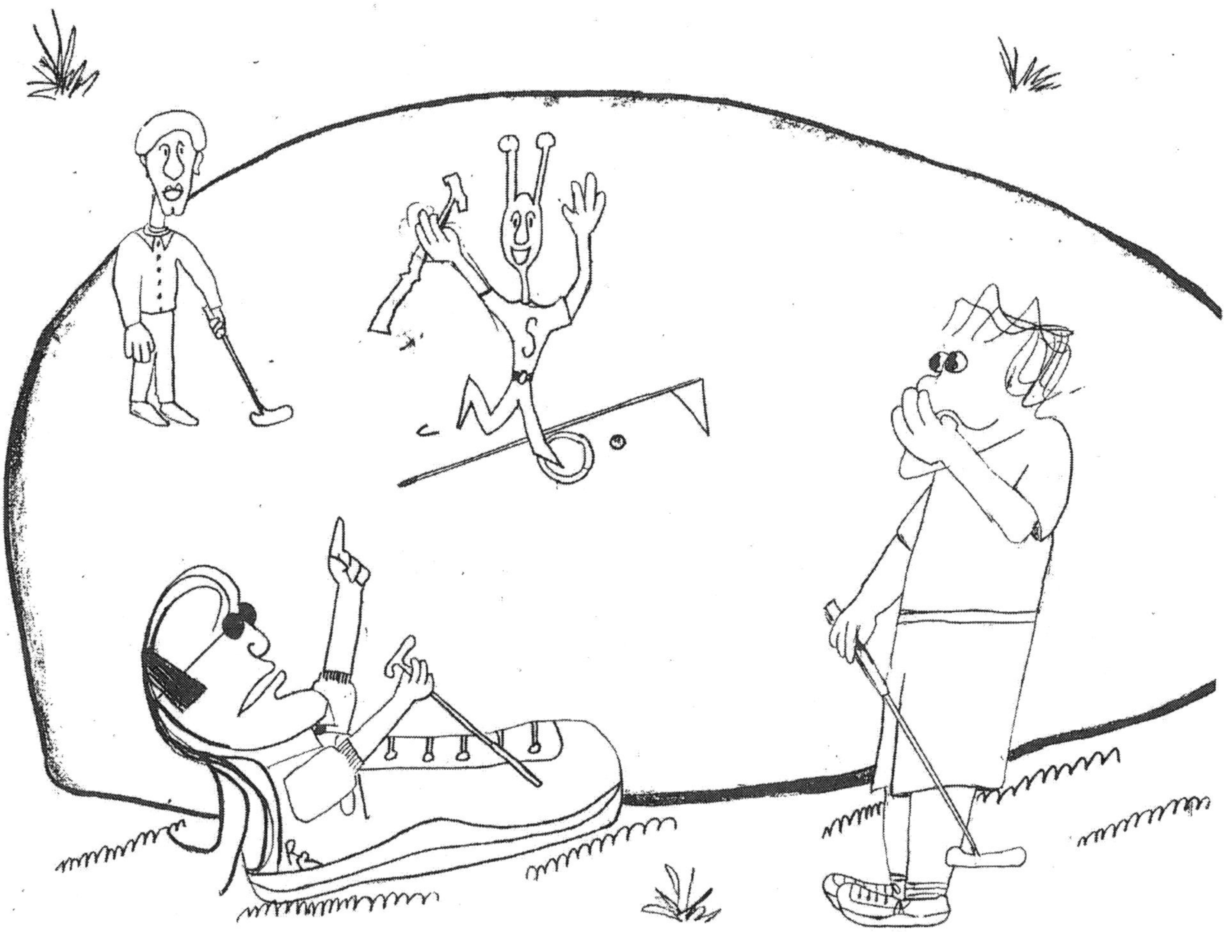

After we finished our chat, Sidney knew that it's courteous to be silent and stand still while others are playing their shots. He learned to walk around the putting lines of others. We showed Sid how to gently put the flagstick back in the hole without ever stepping too close to it. Furthermore, we explained the importance of quickly moving to the next tee before recording the scores. Finally, an explanation of how to replace divots, fix ball marks, and smooth footprints in bunkers completed Sid's lesson on golf manners from yours truly, Rocket Rill.

"We never had to do this stuff on Mars," noted Sidney the Martian.

"Here on Earth, the players are responsible for taking care of the golf course, leaving it *better* than they found it," I lectured, though I think Sidney really enjoyed raking the sand and making the surface smooth for the other players. It was a fun and courteous part of the game.

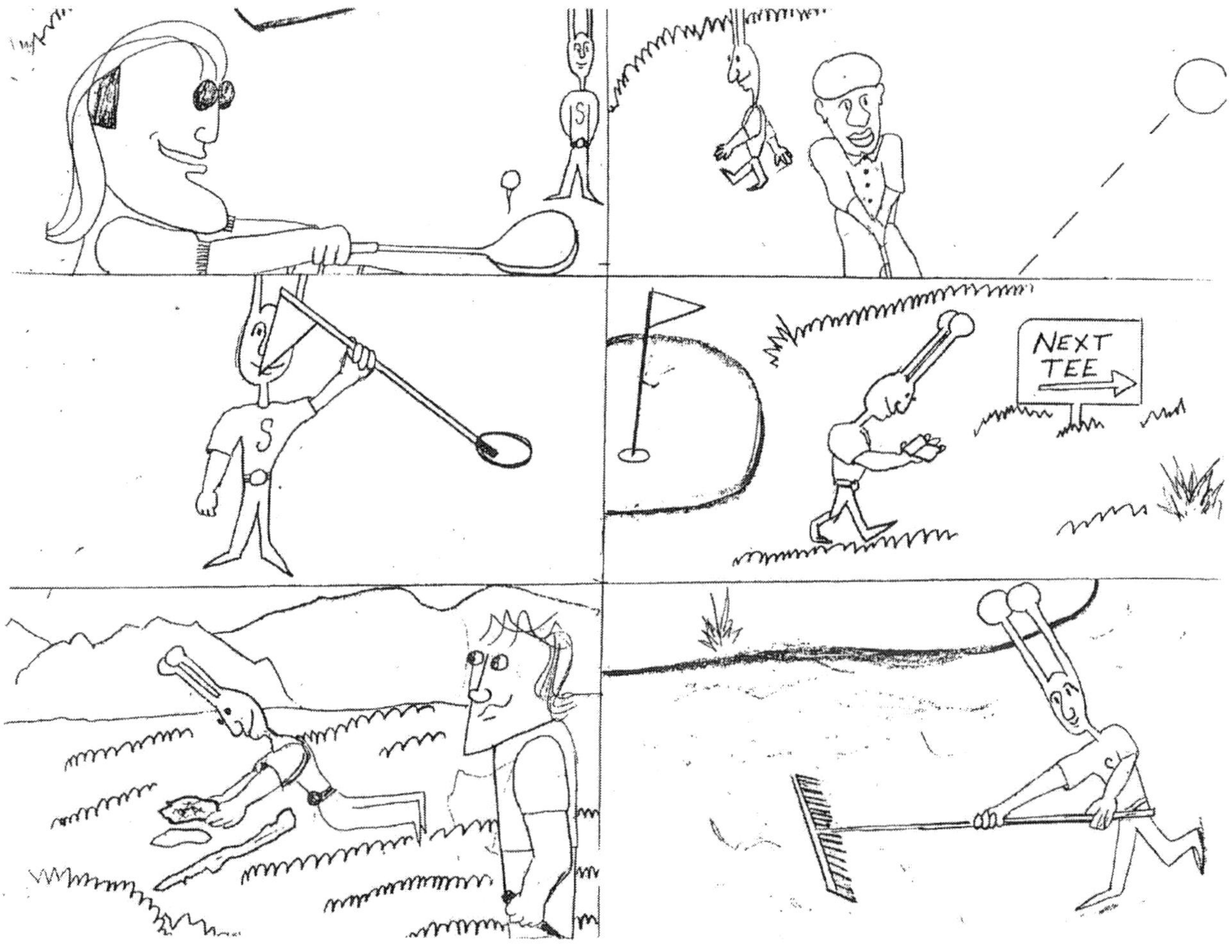
NEXT TEE

"I like taking care of the grounds, and I especially like helping others," said my friend on the way to the clubhouse dining room.

"Fantastic, Sidney. After lunch, we'll replace your sticks with better equipment that fits you, and take a lesson or two with our club pro, Sally Jackson. She knows a lot about the game."

"I just can't wait to start improving," Sidney cried. "Let's go right now!"

"No way Sid, let's eat first. I'm starving!" I said as my stomach growled.

"Mr. Rill, I need to have my golf lesson right away," groaned Sidney.

Today, Sidney learned the importance of safety and punctuality (being on time, even a little early). He learned about the rules and etiquette in the game of golf. And he learned how to take care of the golf course. However, he had yet to learn patience. That was going to take longer than an afternoon.

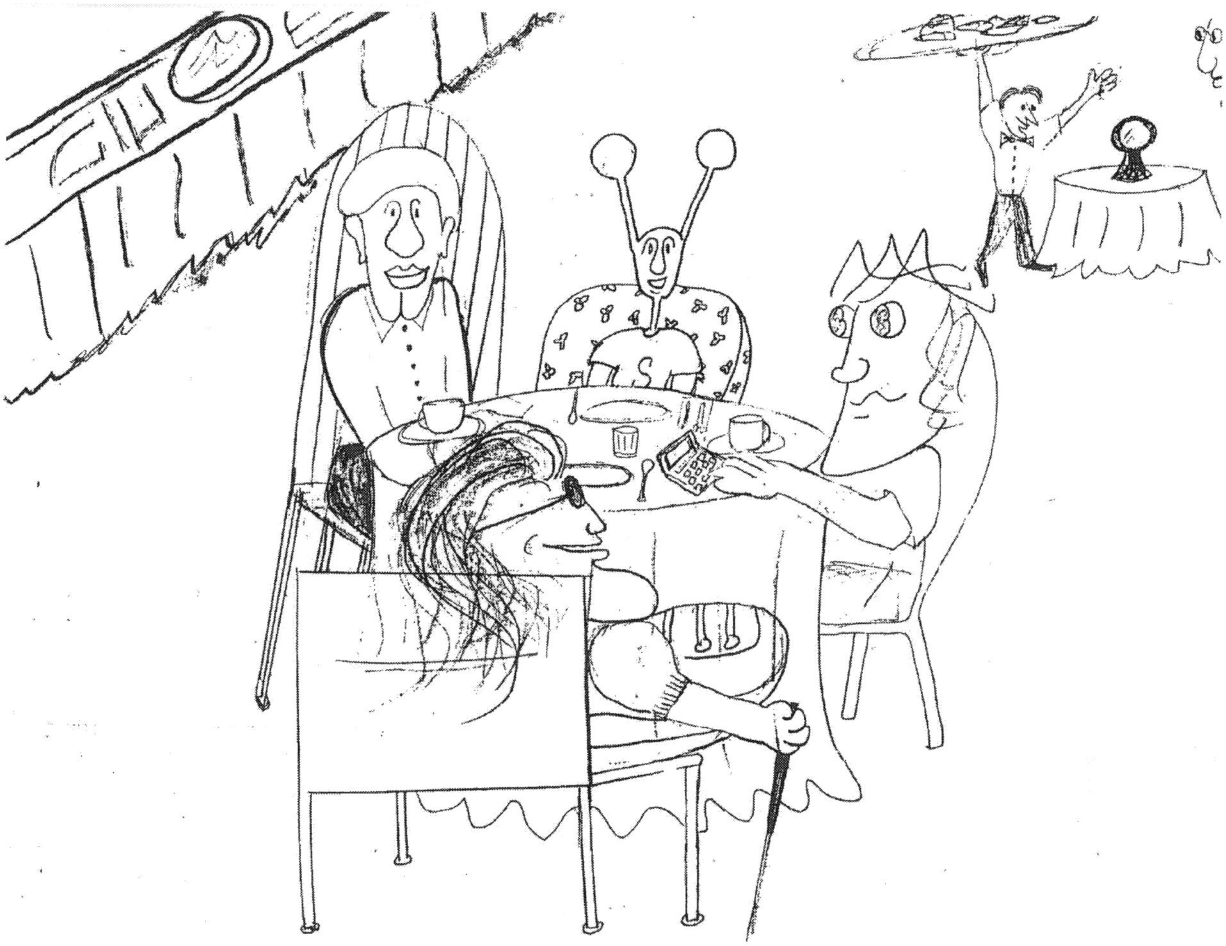

"You have to make an appointment. Sally has a very busy teaching schedule."

"Okay, Mr. Rill. But after my lesson I'm going home to demonstrate to my friends on Mars everything that I've learned on Earth about golf."

I could only imagine what an adventure that would be!

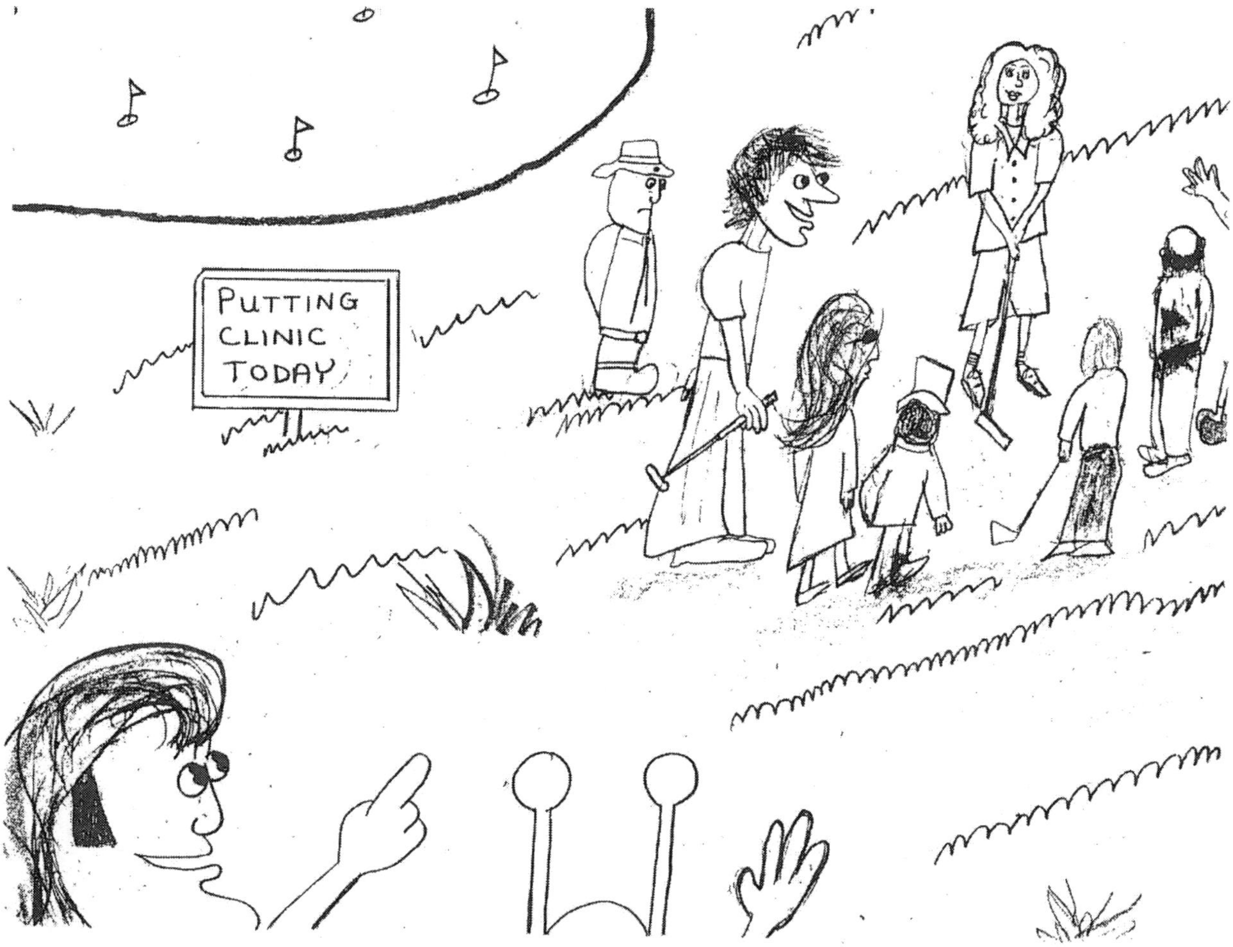
PUTTING
CLINIC
TODAY

"Good luck, Sidney."

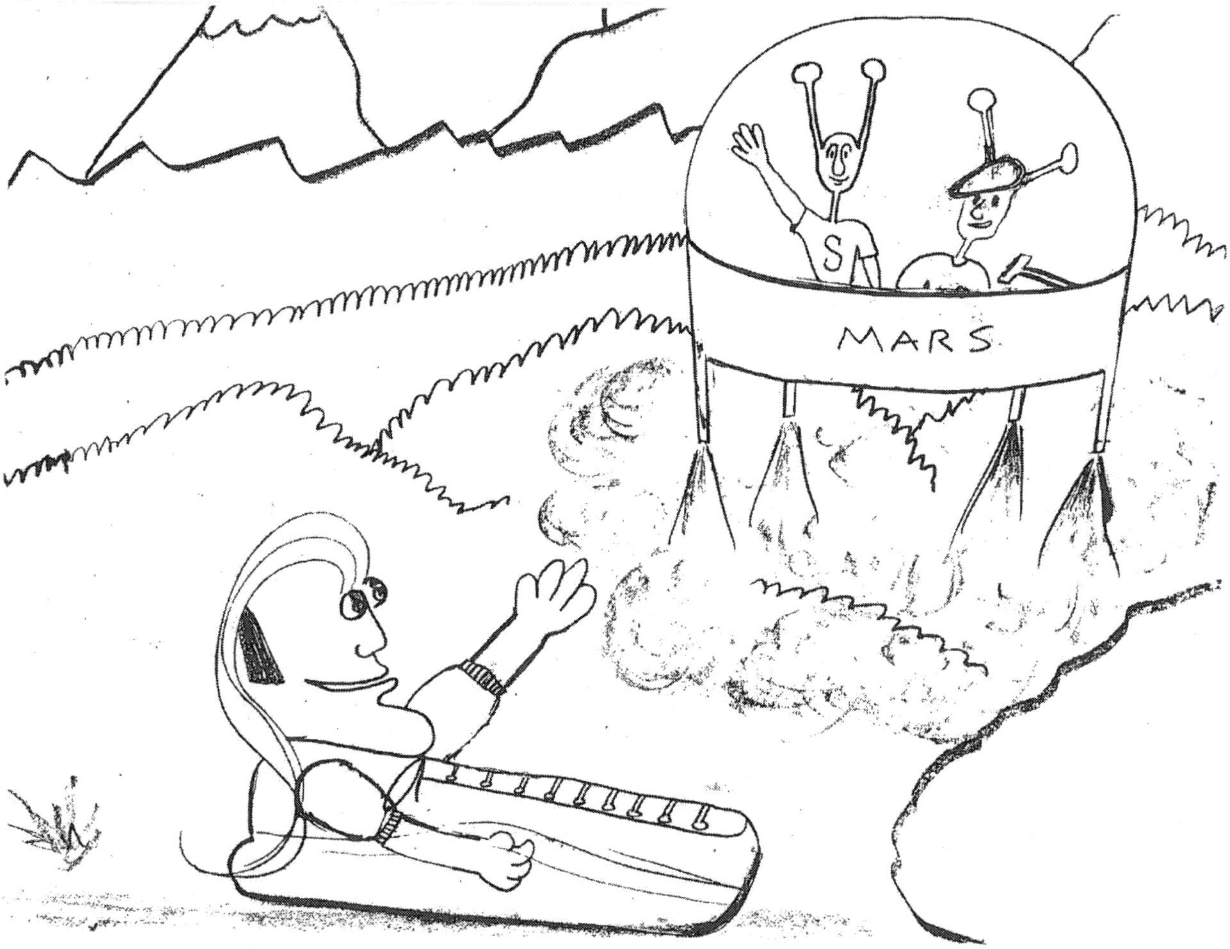
S
MARS

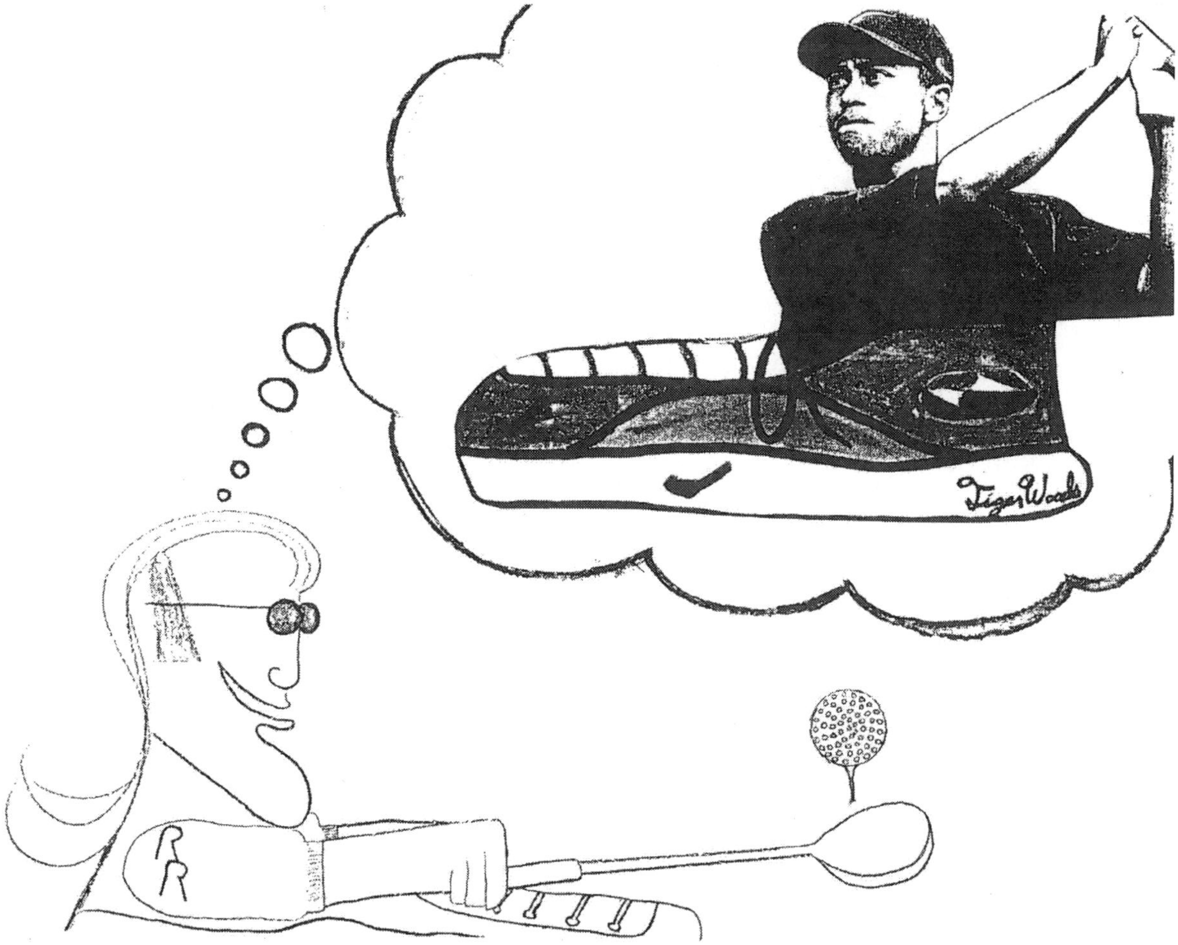
Tiger Woods

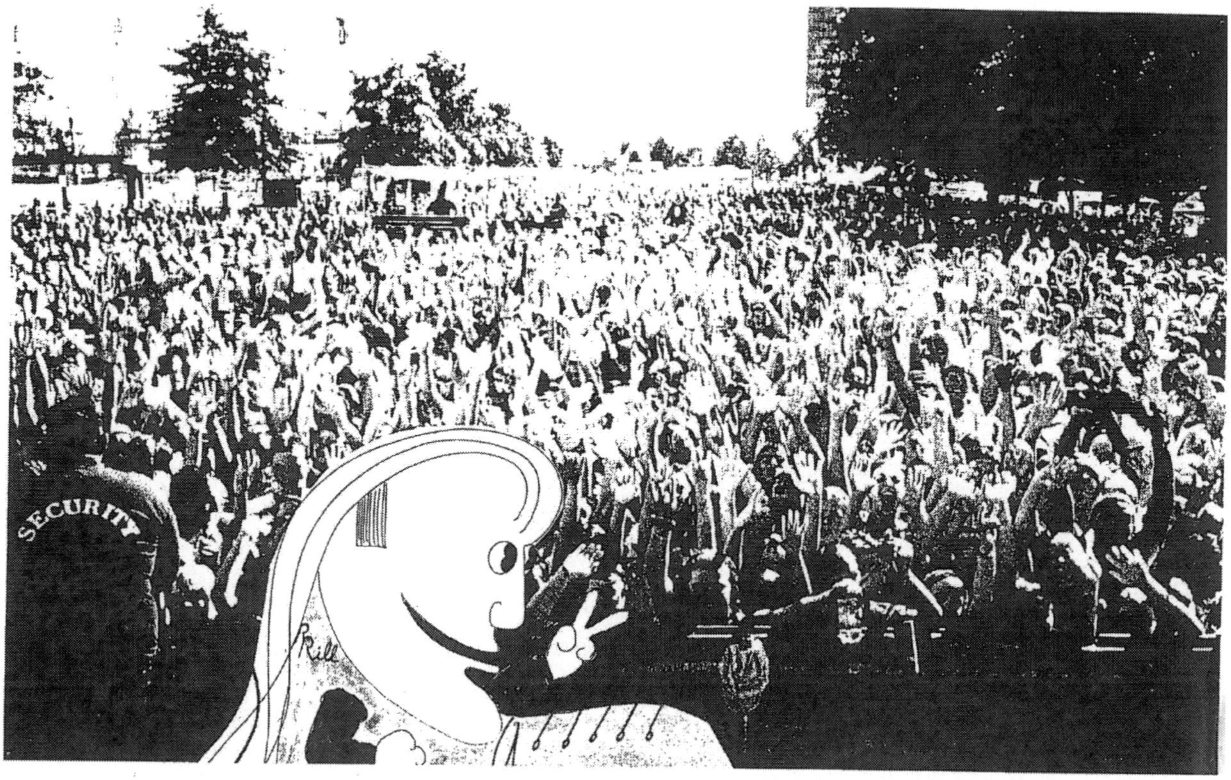
SECURITY

Made in the USA
Coppell, TX
25 January 2022